THE OFFICIAL
NEWCASTLE UNITED
FOOTBALL CLUB
ANNUAL 2006

£6.99

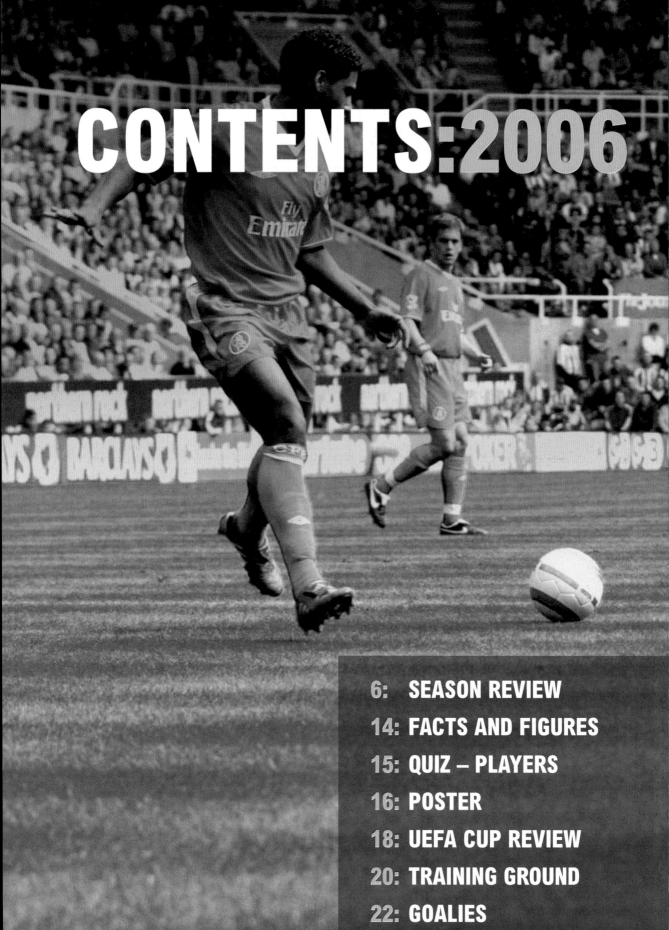

CONTENTS:2006

6: SEASON REVIEW

14: FACTS AND FIGURES

15: QUIZ – PLAYERS

16: POSTER

18: UEFA CUP REVIEW

20: TRAINING GROUND

22: GOALIES

24: QUIZ – EUROPE

25: QUIZ – STRIKERS

26: ALAN SHEARER

30: CLUB HONOURS

32: PLAYER PROFILES

42: WORD SEARCH

44: FA CUP REVIEW

46: JUNIOR MAGPIES

48: KIERON DYER

50: NEW SIGNINGS

52: GRAEME SOUNESS

54: CROSSWORD

56: BACKROOM STAFF

57: UNDER 18s

58: TOP GOALS

60: DID YOU KNOW?

61: QUIZ ANSWERS

SEASON REVIEW

AUGUST 2004

MIDDLESBROUGH 2 NEWCASTLE 2
(Bellamy, Shearer pen)

NEWCASTLE 0 SPURS 1

NEWCASTLE 2 NORWICH CITY 2
(Bellamy, Hughes)

ASTON VILLA 4 NEWCASTLE 2
(Kluivert, O'Brien)

NEWCASTLE United made an unconvincing start to the 2004-5 season and after just four games they parted company with manager Sir Bobby Robson.

Things could hardly have gone much worse for the Magpies in the last four games of Sir Bobby's reign, with the whole club hit by a contagious eye infection ahead of the season opener against Middlesbrough.

Newcastle managed to put a team out and in the end it was referee Steve Bennett's eyes which let him down as television replays showed that Jimmy Floyd Hasselbaink knocked in Boro's 90th minute equaliser with his hand.

United had twice led and in the end it was a case of two points dropped.

Against Spurs in the first home game of the season Newcastle were unfortunate to end up with nothing.

Visiting goalkeeper Paul Robinson kept his first competitive clean sheet since the previous Boxing Day as the visitors went home with all three points thanks to a stunning goal from Timothee Atouba.

United had a chance to put things right against newly-promoted Norwich City at St James' Park four days later, but Robson's team could not pick up that elusive first victory as the Canaries sang all the way home with a point in a 2-2 draw.

Norwich could easily have been singing a lot louder had they taken all three points against a home team that was way out of tune.

So with three games gone - two of them at home and the other at Tyne-Tees rivals Middlesbrough - Newcastle only had two points and were left languishing in 15th in the Premiership.

Things did not get better for Sir Bobby and his team in their next game at Aston Villa, when referee Mike Riley chose not to send off home goalkeeper Thomas Sorensen for a hand ball offence outside the box at the start of the second half.

Robson had controversially left his captain Alan Shearer on the bench and instead gave Patrick Kluivert his first start.

Kluivert got a goal but United still went down 4-2 to Villa and returned to the North East with the worst goals against tally in the Premiership.

United were also in the bottom three and within a week of the defeat at Villa Park they had a new manager, with Graeme Souness replacing Sir Bobby Robson.

SEPTEMBER

NEWCASTLE 3 BLACKBURN 0
(Flitcroft og, Shearer, O'Brien)

SOUTHAMPTON 1 NEWCASTLE 2
(Prutton og, Carr)

NEWCASTLE 3 WEST BROM 1
(Kluivert, Milner, Shearer)

NEW manager Graeme Souness brought with him from Blackburn Rovers his coaching staff, appointing Alan Murray as assistant manager, Dean Saunders as first team coach and Phil Boersma as a coach.

Former first team coach John Carver, however, was given a caretaker's role for the next game because Newcastle United's first match after Souness' appointment was against his former club Blackburn.

Souness watched from the stands at St James' Park as Carver masterminded the Magpies' first win of the season, with Newcastle jumping five places to 12th with a convincing 3-0 victory.

Carver may have been in the home dug-out but there are no prizes for guessing just who the Newcastle players were trying to impress the most of all.

Souness' first game in charge just happened to be against another of his former clubs – Southampton.

United travelled to Southampton knowing that they had not won in the league at the south coast club for 32 years - and came away with a 2-1 victory.

This put Newcastle into eighth position in the Premiership and suddenly things were looking up on Tyneside with West Bromwich Albion the next visitors to St James'.

United ran out 3-1 winners to pick up three Premiership wins in-a-row for the first time in almost a year. It was a good day all-round for Newcastle with Patrick Kluivert scoring his first league goal in front of his own fans while James Milner managed to score his first goal in a black and white shirt.

Souness and his team moved up to sixth in the table – but no one would have guessed that they would not go any higher for the rest of the season.

OCTOBER

BIRMINGHAM 2 NEWCASTLE 2
(Jenas, Butt)

CHARLTON 1 NEWCASTLE 1
(Bellamy)

NEWCASTLE 4 MAN CITY 3
(Robert, Shearer pen, Elliott, Bellamy)

BOLTON 2 NEWCASTLE 1
(Ambrose)

NEWCASTLE United were full of optimism at the start of a new month - and they were to go through it unbeaten until the very last day.

After the heat of Tel Aviv in the UEFA Cup Souness and his team left a grey St Andrews having taken a point from Birmingham City. Despite their tiring trip to Israel the Magpies fought City all the way in a real belter of a game.

And the feeling in the Newcastle camp was that it was a point gained rather than two points lost, despite having taken a third minute lead through Jermaine Jenas.

United's other goal came from Nicky Butt, the former Manchester United midfielder opening his account with a spectacular scissor kick.

Newcastle were not on duty for another fortnight because of the international matches and they had lost a bit of their edge in the 1-1 draw with Charlton Athletic at The Valley.

Craig Bellamy got the United goal but spoilt things with his reaction to his substitution by Graeme Souness.

All this was forgotten in the next Premiership match when Bellamy put away an 89th minute winner in the thrilling 4-3 victory over Manchester City at St James' Park.

Man City manager Kevin Keegan, who suffered a famous 4-3 defeat at Anfield while

Newcastle boss, took it on the chin.

But United themselves suffered a body blow when their 10-match unbeaten league and cup run came to an end when they went down 2-1 to Bolton Wanderers at the Reebok Stadium.

Newcastle could not cope with Bolton's aggressive style of play and both Bolton's goals came from dead ball situations.

In contrast United's equaliser from Darren Ambrose was struck from 30-yards and was a candidate for goal of the season.

It was Newcastle's third successive defeat at the stadium, and as a result United slipped down to eighth place in the table.

NOVEMBER

NEWCASTLE 1 FULHAM 4
(Bellamy)

NEWCASTLE 1 MANCHESTER UNITED 3
(Shearer)

CRYSTAL PALACE 0 NEWCASTLE 2
(Kluivert, Bellamy)

NEWCASTLE 1 EVERTON 1
(Bellamy)

AFTER their first defeat in 11 matches, Newcastle United desperately needed to get back to winning ways when Fulham arrived at St James' Park at the start of November.

If one game summed up the Magpies' Premiership season, however, then it was the visit of the Cottagers.

Seemingly each time Fulham attacked they scored, while their goalkeeper Mark Crossley later admitted he had one of his best-ever games.

At one stage the Londoners were leading a shell-shocked Newcastle 4-0, and Craig Bellamy's consolation was greeted by near silence by the home fans.

Steve Harper was in the United goal for his first Premiership appearance in four years, with No. 1 goalkeeper Shay Given away on paternity leave.

Newcastle, knocked out of the Carling Cup in midweek, then faced Manchester United at St James'.

Sir Alex Ferguson's team won 3-1, with a well-taken goal from Alan Shearer providing little consolation.

Shearer was missing for the next match at Crystal Palace with a thigh injury, which kept him out until the middle of January.So United had a new strike force for the game with Crystal Palace at Selhurst Park in Patrick Kluivert and Craig Bellamy and both scored in the last 11 minutes in a 2-0 victory.

It was their first clean sheet of the season away from St James' in the Premiership and Newcastle also maintained their record of having scored in every game on their travels.

Graeme Souness' team, however, were unable to cash in on a rare away win when Everton came to St James' the following weekend.

United dominated the game after taking a fifth minute lead through Bellamy, but could not score a second goal and Everton took a point home thanks to a Lee Carsley free kick.

DECEMBER

CHELSEA 4 NEWCASTLE 0

NEWCASTLE 1 PORTSMOUTH 1
(Bowyer)

LIVERPOOL 3 NEWCASTLE 1
(Kluivert)

BLACKBURN 2 NEWCASTLE 2
(Dyer, Robert)

ARSENAL 1 NEWCASTLE 0

NEWCASTLE United matched Premiership leaders Chelsea all the way at Stamford Bridge for the first hour, but still left London on the wrong end of a 4-0 defeat.

Frank Lampard opened the floodgates in the 63rd minute and Chelsea's 89th and 90th minute goals from Arjen Robben and Marteja

Kezman gave the scoreline a lop-sided look.

The result saw the Magpies slip down to 12th in the Premiership – their lowest placing since Graeme Souness took charge.

Newcastle had failed to get the defeat out of their systems when Portsmouth came to St James' Park a week later.

Once again United had the boost of an early goal when Lee Bowyer lashed the ball into the Pompey net from 20 yards after only three minutes.

Portsmouth, however, had plenty of players who had plenty to prove including former Magpies striker Lomana LuaLua and Geordie Steve Stone.

It was Stone, born across the River Tyne in Gateshead, who earned Portsmouth a well-deserved point with his 29th minute equaliser. His shot took a wicked deflection off home skipper Jermaine Jenas.

As Portsmouth started the long journey back to the south coast Newcastle were left to reflect on the fact that they had gone four League games in a row in front of their own supporters without a victory.

United had two trips to the North West over Christmas and they brought home just one point from the 2-2 draw with Souness' former club Blackburn Rovers at Ewood Park, which followed a 3-1 defeat to Liverpool at Anfield.

Newcastle had never won at Blackburn in the Premiership and they must have thought they were in with a great chance when they were twice in front.

United ended the year with a 1-0 home defeat by Arsenal at St James' Park - but they got a lot of their pride back.

The Arsenal goal in first-half injury time came when Patrick Vieira's shot looped into the net courtesy of a deflection off Jermaine Jenas.

Newcastle felt that they had been hard done by when Ashley Cole handled in the penalty area, but referee Steve Bennett and his assistant were the only people at St James' not to see it.

JANUARY 2005

NEWCASTLE 2 BIRMINGHAM CITY 1
(Ameobi, Bowyer)
WEST BROM 0 NEWCASTLE 0
NEWCASTLE 2 SOUTHAMPTON 1
(Shearer pen, Bramble)
ARSENAL 1 NEWCASTLE 0

NEWCASTLE United started the New Year with a 2-1 victory over Birmingham City - their first in six Premiership matches.

Lee Bowyer's winner was the Magpies' 700th goal in the Premiership and Shola Ameobi's opener was his first goal of the season in the league.

Newcastle had their new transfer window signings - £8m Jean Alain Boumsong and Celestine Babayaro - in the crowd and the pair saw the players in their positions turn in fine displays.

United's first trip of the Year pitted them with West Bromwich Albion at The Hawthorns and neither side could find the back of the net in a disappointing goalless draw.

Newcastle had enough of the play and chances to win half a dozen matches and the only plus point - apart from the point that is – was that they kept only their third Premiership clean sheet of the season.

They say that a point away from home is a good one but Graeme Souness looked down in the dumps as he left The Hawthorns.

Newcastle welcomed back Alan Shearer for the first time since the home defeat by Manchester United in the middle of November, when his former team Southampton made the long trek to Tyneside.

And within nine minutes Shearer had knocked in a penalty as he led Newcastle to a 2-1 victory.

Defenders Boumsong and Babayaro also impressed on their home debuts, while Titus Bramble scored United's second.

Newcastle's next port of call was North London for the return game with Arsenal at Highbury and after a row with Graeme Souness Craig Bellamy was left out of the startling line up.

A sullen Bellamy watched the game from the bench as United were well beaten, with the 1-0 scoreline flattering the Magpies.

They rallied in the final 10 minutes, however, and the Arsenal fans were screaming at referee Steve Dunn to blow the final whistle.

Within a week Bellamy had been loaned to Celtic for the rest of the season.

UEFA Cup and Chelsea out of the FA Cup Newcastle took their revenge on Bolton Wanderers for their 2-1 loss at the Reebok Stadium in October with victory by the same scoreline at St James' Park.

Bolton arrived on Tyneside as the Premiership's form team but their poor record at St James' Park continued.

It was Newcastle's fifth win out of six home Premiership games with Bolton, the other being drawn, and nobody was more delighted than Kieron Dyer, who scored the winner for United.

FEBRUARY

MANCHESTER CITY 1 NEWCASTLE 1

NEWCASTLE 1 CHARLTON 1

NEWCASTLE 2 BOLTON 1

United's game against Manchester City at the beginning of February will be remembered for one thing – Alan Shearer's 250th Premiership goal.

Shearer became the first player to reach the milestone and with his rivals still short of the 200-goal mark it will stand for some time.

However the goal was to be his last league goal of the season, though he continued to score in Europe.

Kieron Dyer, a player who would love to score more goals, grabbed only his second Premiership goal of the season in the disappointing 1-1 home draw with Charlton Athletic.

The result saw Graeme Souness's men continue to hover around 12th place, unable to break into the top half of the table.

They did have one break - a training camp in the sunshine of Dubai - and the Magpies came back and promptly won eight games in a row.

Indeed after knocking Heerenveen out of the

MARCH

NEWCASTLE 1 LIVERPOOL 0
(Robert)

PORTSMOUTH 1 NEWCASTLE 1
(Dyer)

WHEN Newcastle United beat Liverpool 1-0 at St James' Park at the beginning of March it was the first time they had won by that scoreline in the Premiership this season.

It was the Magpies' fifth successive victory and stretched their unbeaten run to eight games.

Not only that, it was also Newcastle's 200th win in the Premiership and the Toon Army went home happy.

But no-one was happier than Newcastle's left winger Laurent Robert, who has always managed to score goals against Liverpool. His latest goal was extra special, with the Frenchman scoring a brilliant 70th minute free-kick.

It was also an extra-special day for manager Graeme Souness as it was his first victory in 13 attempts as a manager over the club he first played for and then managed.

If Robert and Souness were happy, then so to was keeper Shay Given. It was only the second time United had kept a clean sheet against Liverpool in 22 Premiership matches.

Funnily enough the other occasion was also at St James' in the 2002-03 season, when Robert again curled in the only goal of the game direct from a free-kick.

Newcastle headed off to the south coast in good heart looking for a record-breaking ninth win in a row in all competitions but they did not get it as they played out a 1-1 draw with Portsmouth at Fratton Park.

Kieron Dyer gave Newcastle the lead but they were again denied by Pompey's Gateshead-born midfielder Steve Stone.

While Newcastle may not have got the win they were looking for, at least they were still unbeaten in 12 matches.

APRIL

NEWCASTLE 0 ASTON VILLA 3

SPURS 1 NEWCASTLE 0

NORWICH 2 NEWCASTLE 1
(Kluivert)

MAN UTD 2 NEWCASTLE 1
(Ambrose)

NEWCASTLE 0 MIDDLESBROUGH 0

NEWCASTLE 0 CRYSTAL PALACE 0

WITH Newcastle United in the quarter-finals of the UEFA Cup and semi-final of the FA Cup there was an air of anticipation at the beginning of April.

Graeme Souness, however, must have thought it was an April fool when Lee Bowyer and Kieron Dyer were sent off for fighting each other in the 3-0 home defeat to Aston Villa.

The day was supposed to be a celebration after skipper Alan Shearer had announced he was going to play on for another season, but in the end Villa deservedly went home with all three points.

It was only their second-ever win on Tyneside in the Premiership.

Newcastle had Steve Harper in goal for the injured Shay Given against Spurs at White Hart Lane in the next game, and Newcastle's longest-serving player was guilty of the mistake which saw Jermain Defoe score the only goal of the game just before the interval.

After going out of the UEFA Cup and the FA Cup to Sporting Lisbon and Manchester United in the space of four days, United had another frustrating night when they were beaten 2-1 by Norwich City at Carrow Road.

Patrick Kluivert looked as though he had saved Newcastle a point when he came on as a substitute and equalised in the 90th minute, only for Norwich to go straight down the other end and snatch a sensational winner.

Newcastle were at a low ebb, and short of nine players, when they travelled to meet Manchester United at Old Trafford just seven days after the Red Devils had knocked them out of the FA Cup.

However they turned in a spirited show and actually took the lead through Darren Ambrose.

It took a wonder goal from Wayne Rooney to put Man United back in the game and defender Wes Brown grabbed a rather undeserved winning goal.

The end of the season could now not come quick enough for United and they played out two home goalless draws in the space of four days with Middlesbrough and Crystal Palace.

MAY

FULHAM 1 NEWCASTLE 3
(Ambrose, Kluivert, Ameobi)

EVERTON 2 NEWCASTLE 0

NEWCASTLE 1 CHELSEA 1
(Geremi og)

AN under-strength Newcastle United went to Craven Cottage looking for their first win in the Premiership in eight games and they got it with a well-deserved 3-1 victory over Fulham.

Patrick Kluivert, who was to be released at the end of the season, reflected on what

might have been with a goal and a more than useful performance.

Shola Ameobi too had cause to celebrate with just his second Premiership goal of the season.

The only pity was that Tomasz Radzinski's late consolation for Fulham not only spoilt what would have been a deserved clean sheet for the third game in a row for Shay Given, but it also robbed the Magpies of equalling their best ever League result at Craven Cottage.

Newcastle completed their away programme against Everton at Goodison Park, and Graeme Souness must have wondered just how the Merseysiders and not United were going to finish in fourth place and earn a spot in the Champions League qualifiers.

Newcastle outplayed Everton in the first half but missed chance after chance and the travelling supporters watched as the Goodison Park outfit hit back through a set piece.

The game was over 11 minutes into the second half when Shola Ameobi reacted to a foul and was sent off, with Everton going on to record only their third win over United in the Premiership at Goodison Park.

New champions Chelsea brought the curtain down on another season at St James' Park and once again Newcastle showed that they can live with the best of teams on their day in the 1-1 draw.

United, who had not managed a home goal in the Premiership since the win over Liverpool on March 5, got an own goal against Chelsea.

Newcastle came off expecting to finish their season in 12th place but they found that Birmingham City had scored a last minute winner against Arsenal and that by beating Norwich City 6-0 Fulham had a better goal difference.

In the end the Magpies finished 14th in the Premiership table and undoubtedly their 19-game cup programme - half a league season - had taken its toll.

ST. JAMES' PARK
FACTS AND FIGURES

CAPACITY:

Sir John Hall Stand:	20,145
Milburn Stand:	14,929
South Stand:	12,043
East Stand:	5,240
Television podiums:	30
TOTAL:	**52,387**
Wheelchair spaces:	187
Family area seats:	844
Executive Boxes:	82

CONFERENCE AND BANQUETING FACILITIES:
Catering for 4,500 in varied size rooms, the facilities are the largest in the North East.

MATCH DAY: 4,500 meals, 10,000 teas/coffees, 5,000 pies/chips, 30 cases of Newcastle Brown Ale, 500 bottles of wine and 200 bottles of champagne are served by around 800 staff.

CAR PARKING: Two multi-storey car parks adjacent/attached to stadium

LENGTH OF CANTILEVER ROOF: 65.5m (one of the largest in the world). The distance from the highest seat to the pitch is 69m. The commentary gantry is 20m high.

FLOODLIGHTS: 66 on East Stand and 102 on Milburn Stand.

STEEL TONNAGE: 7000 tonnes

TRANSPARENT ROOF: 16,200 square metres (equivalent size of two football pitches).

QUIZ:1 PLAYERS

1 Newcastle signed Kieron Dyer, Titus Bramble and Darren Ambrose from the same club. Which one?

2 Where was Shola Ameobi born?

3 Which member is Newcastle's most capped player? He's in the current squad.

4 Who was Newcastle's captain when Alan Shearer was injured halfway through last season?

5 From which club did Newcastle sign Jean Alain Boumsong?

6 Newcastle midfielder Amdy Faye plays for which country?

7 Robbie Elliott has played for one other team apart from Newcastle. Which one?

8 He was born in Dublin in August 1976. Apart from Newcastle he has had only one other club. Who is he?

9 This player has the unusual middle name of Malachi. Who is he?

10 What nationality is Newcastle midfielder Charles N'Zogbia?

Answers on p61

UEFA CUP REVIEW

AFTER reaching the semi-finals of the UEFA cup the previous season Newcastle United were hoping to go one better in the 2004-5 campaign.

They had a new formula to contend with after the first round, switching from a knockout to a League with five teams. However it wasn't a case of home or away but two away and two at home.

United found themselves breaking new ground when they were drawn against Israeli League outfit Hapeol Bnei Sakhnin in their first game. They were duly despatched 2-0 with Patrick Kluivert scoring both goals.

Because they could not handle the visit of United and their fans the return leg was switched from Sakhnin's small and compact stadium to Israel's national Ramat Gan Stadium in Tel Aviv.

United found this to their liking, doing a very professional job with skipper Alan Shearer grabbing only the second hat-trick of his career in Europe and Kluivert weighing in with another couple of goals in a 5-1 win.

This took Newcastle into the group stage and as in the case of Israel they played their first European match in Greece against tiny Panionios in Athens.

Newcastle weren't at their best but they still picked up three points with a 1-0 victory thanks to a late Alan Shearer penalty won by substitute Shola Ameobi.

This brought United into opposition with a side from Georgia for the first time and Dinamo Tbilisi were beaten 2-0 at St James' Park.

So with four games in Europe Newcastle had won them all, scoring 10 goals and only conceding one.

To be fair the opposition had not been great but the general consensus of opinion was that Newcastle would face tougher opposition when they travelled to France to meet Sochaux. Indeed – but for keeper Shay Given in his 300th game for Newcastle Graeme Souness's side could easily have been in trouble. But once Lee Bowyer had put Newcastle into the lead in the 29th minute the floodgates opened and they roared to a 4-0 victory.

The win in France meant that Newcastle only needed a point from their last match against Sporting Lisbon to go through to the next stage - and they got it in a rather uninspiring 1-1 draw.

There was a two month winter break from the UEFA Cup but when the competition resumed Newcastle were pitted with Dutch side Heerenveen from whom they had signed Danish striker Jon Dahl Tomasson in Kenny Dalglish's days as manager.

As in the game in France Newcastle did not get off to a very good start in the Abe Lenstra Stadion. But after going a goal down midway though the first half Graeme Souness sent on Laurent Robert as a substitute for Shola Ameobi and the Frenchman turned the game as he helped make goals for Alan Shearer and Lee Bowyer and a 2-1 away victory was secured.

When Newcastle won the second leg by a similar score at St James' Park it meant that for the first time in their history the club went into March still involved in two cup competitions as they were still going strong in the FA Cup.

What it also meant was that Newcastle would play their 100th game in Europe when top Greek side Olympiakos came to St James' Park. First Newcastle had to go to Athens for the second time in the season in the UEFA Cup and if they did not sparkle against Panionios they certainly demolished an Olympiakos side which earlier in the campaign had been only a couple of minutes away from knocking the

RESULTS

NEWCASTLE 2 SAKHNIN 0
(16.9.04 Kluivert 2)

SAKHNIN 1 NEWCASTLE 5
(30.09.04 Kluivert 2, Shearer 3)

PANIONIOS 0 NEWCASTLE 1
(21.10.04 Shearer pen)

NEWCASTLE 2 DINAMO TBILISI 0
(04.11.04 Shearer, Bellamy)

SOCHAUX 0 NEWCASTLE 4
(25.11.04 Bowyer, Ameobi, Bellamy, Robert)

NEWCASTLE 1 SPORTING LISBON 1
(16.12.04 Bellamy)

HEERENVEEN 1 NEWCASTLE 2
(17.02.05 Shearer, Bowyer)

NEWCASTLE 2 HEERENVEEN 1
(24.02.05 Breuer og, Shearer)

OLYMPIAKOS 1 NEWCASTLE 3
(10.03.05 Shearer pen, Robert, Kluivert)

NEWCASTLE 4 OLYMPIAKOS 0
(16.03.05 Dyer, Shearer 2, Bowyer)

NEWCASTLE 1 SPORTING LISBON 0
(07.04.05 Shearer)

SPORTING LISBON 4 NEWCASTLE 1
(14.04.05 Dyer)

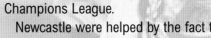

eventual winners Liverpool out of the Champions League.

Newcastle were helped by the fact that Olympiakos had two players sent off in the first half and while they could have made the second leg at St James' Park a formality no-one was complaining at the 3-1 away victory.

The second leg was United's tenth game in Europe and they made it win number 9 in their 100th appearance, beating the Greeks 4-0 and going through to the quarter-finals of the UEFA Cup in what can only be described as a remarkable 7-1 aggregate.

Newcastle again found themselves up against Sporting Lisbon, this time in a two legged battle for a place in the semi-finals for the second successive season.

The Portuguese outfit had beaten Middlesbrough in the previous round and while skipper Alan Shearer gave Newcastle a deserved 1-0 home win Graeme Souness's side missed several easy chances on the night - something they were going to regret a week later in Lisbon.

Yet when Kieron Dyer gave Newcastle a 20th minute lead in Lisbon it looked all over - but Sporting had other ideas and all credit to them.

They ran in no fewer than four goals amid ecstatic scenes in the Jose Alvalade Stadium to go through to the semi-finals at Newcastle's expense.

It was probably Newcastle's most disappointing night of the season. They had played 12 games in Europe, winning 10 of them and only losing that last one in Lisbon.

Despite this and the fact that they had scored twice as many goals in the UEFA Cup as they had conceded the Newcastle United players were inconsolable after the game in Lisbon.

They had put in a tremendous effort in the UEFA Cup. But it just wasn't good enough.

TRAINING GROUND

NEWCASTLE United's state-of-the-art training facilities are among the best in the country, the club having invested heavily in its first ever permanent base.

The Magpies had never had their own training complex until 2003, when the club moved into brand new facitilies in Benton and Little Benton.

Having trained at a windswept Benwell and on hired pitches at Durham City and Chester-le-Street in recent years, chairman Freddy Shepherd was determined that Newcastle United should finally have a place called home.

When a proud Shepherd unveiled the Newcastle United Training Centre and adjacent Academy, he said: "It has taken us 110 years to get all of this."

There is a full-size indoor hall and 13 all-weather and two floodlit outdoor pitches across the two sites, meaning Newcastle United can train whatever the weather.

Previously, bad weather had often disrupted training and match preparation.

Now thanks to the huge indoor hall, which measures 96m x 68m and is the biggest of its kind in Europe, that is a thing on the past.

An incredible 144,000 tonnes of earth was moved and laid, and more than 14 miles of drains were sunk beneath the pitches to ensure they are never waterlogged.

Also on the North Tyneside sites are gyms, restaurants and treatment rooms for the club's footballers, with everything geared towards first team success on the football pitch.

The facilities have also been used by the Newcastle Falcons rugby team, and Durham and England cricketer Steve Harmison, himself a Magpies fan.

GOALIES

IS Shay Given the greatest ever goalkeeper to play for Newcastle United?

That's a question that must be on the lips of Newcastle fans as the Irishman continues to turn in top class performances at St James' Park.

Certainly Paul Joannou, Newcastle's club historian and statistician, is convinced Given is getting closer to being the No 1 keeper although at the moment he puts him in fourth place. Paul, who knows everything there is to know about Newcastle United, says:

"If Shay Given continues in the next two or three years as he has in the past two or three years he could well go on and be regarded as the best goalkeeper the club has ever had.

"There are a lot of things to be taken into consideration when you try to dig deep and find out just who are the club's greatest ever players.

"Length of service comes into it and what they have won for the club. And so too does whether they are an international player or not and of course an important factor is the player's actual ability." Looking at Shay Given he is starting to fit nicely into these categories. He has been with Newcastle since 1997-98 and he has played over 250 games for the club.

"Presuming he stays then in the next five years he is going to have well over 400 appearances to his name and don't forget he is now the most capped player Newcastle have had on their books."

Newcastle of course are renowned for having some of the greatest centre forwards this country has ever seen - Alan Shearer, Hughie Gallacher, Jackie Milburn and Malcolm Macdonald. They have had some truly fine full-backs but you can count on one hand the number of excellent goalkeepers the club have had. Indeed Paul Joannou adds: "In their 100-year history Newcastle have only had a select group of goalkeepers who can be said to be really outstanding and Shay Given is among them.

"Really goalkeeper has been one of our weakest positions but we have still had some truly excellent keepers. Jimmy Lawrence from the Edwardian era who won five FA Cup medals, three League championships and played over 500 games would be my choice as our top keeper.

"I would put Ronnie Simpson who played in two FA Cup finals at No 2. And while this may surprise a lot of people Willie McFaul would be my No 3.

"After that you have got to look at keepers who did not come into the great category but who had reasonable spells at the club like Albert McInroy, Mick Mahoney and Pavel Srnicek. I would rate Shay Given above these and at the moment I would place him in fourth spot behind Jimmy Lawrence, Ronnie Simpson and Willie McFaul.

"But in the next couple of years I expect Shay Given to emerge as the greatest ever Newcastle United goalkeeper."

QUIZ:2 EUROPE

1 Which French team did Newcastle beat in the UEFA Cup last season?

2 Only one Newcastle player has topped over 50 games for the club in Europe. Who is he?

3 Newcastle have played over 100 games in Europe. True or false?

4 This young player got his first taste in senior football in an UEFA Cup tie in Majorca in March 2004. Name him.

5 Which club has Newcastle played more than any other in Europe?

6 How many times have Newcastle played in the Champions League?

7 At the start of this season he was on 23. But he has 10 goals for Newcastle in Europe. Who is he?

8 When he came on as substitute for Newcastle against Olympiakos at St James' Park last season this player was making his debut for the club. Name him.

9 Which team knocked Newcastle out of the UEFA Cup in 2003-4?

10 Who were Newcastle's first ever opponents in Europe?

Answers on p61

QUIZ:3 STRIKERS

1 Name the Columbian striker signed from Parma by Kevin Keegan in 1996?

2 Newcastle United signed forward Paul Kitson from which club?

3 Name the Danish striker signed from Dutch club Heerenveen in 1997.

4 Alan Shearer's first Premiership goal for Newcastle United came against which team?

5 How many goals did Craig Bellamy score in his first season at St James' Park?

6 Andy Cole scored a club record 41 goals for Newcastle United in which season?

7 Les Ferdinand scored against which club on his Newcastle United debut?

8 Name the forward signed by Newcastle United from Lincoln City in November 1995.

9 Michael Chopra spent the 2004/05 season on loan at which League One club?

10 Newcastle United signed which striker from Wimbledon in July 2000?

11 Duncan Ferguson joined Newcastle United from which club in 1998?

12 Paul Robinson's only Newcastle United goal came against which European club?

13 Which all-time Newcastle United great played for both Merseyside clubs between his two spells at St James' Park?

14 Name the striker signed from Colchester United in September 2000.

15 Kevin Keegan signed which striker from Millwall in August 1993?

Answers on p61

SHEARER

IT'S one of the most famous shirts in football ... the Newcastle United No 9 jersey. And it will be worn for the last time this season by the legendary Alan Shearer.

After announcing he would retire at the end of last season Shearer did something he has rarely done before ... he changed his mind.

And they were dancing in the streets of Newcastle at the news their talisman skipper was going to play on for one more season. Now Shearer will be looking to make his last season a memorable one.

He started the season as the greatest goalscorer in the history of the Premiership with exactly 250 goals – 76 more than his nearest rival Andy Cole who is the same age as the 35-year-old Newcastle skipper and not a threat. And Robbie Fowler who stands third in the Premiership goals rankings started the season 97 goals behind Shearer and unlikely to get to the 250 mark.

Shearer also has the most hat-tricks in the Premiership - 11 to Fowler's nine - and when he scored against Manchester City at St James' Park in January 2003 after only 10 seconds it equalled the fastest goal in the Premiership's history. No wonder Sky Television's front man Martin Tyler says quite simply: "Alan Shearer is the greatest player the Premiership has ever had." And Newcastle chairman Freddy Shepherd chips in by saying: "Alan Shearer is the greatest player this football club has ever had."

But Shearer knows that past achievements will not mean a thing as he

strives to help Newcastle get the trophy and success their fans deserve in his last season in that No 9 black and white shirt.

It has been said in some quarters that Newcastle and Shearer had a bad time last season. But they did reach the semi-final of the FA Cup and the last eight of the UEFA Cup.

And despite being out injured for a couple of months Shearer still helped himself to 19 goals ... more than Didier Drogba and Eidur Gudjohnsen at Chelsea, Manchester United pair Wayne Rooney and Ruud van Nistelrooy and Jimmy Floyd Hasselbaink at Middlesbrough.

But Shearer knows better than anyone that his past achievements count for nothing and that it's a brand new ball game in the new season. And he also knows it is not getting any easier, claiming that last season was one of the longest and hardest of his career.

But like every other Premiership player Shearer has had some sun on his back and he will be raring to go again. He will treat his last season like he has every other since he broke into the Southampton team as a teenager - by never failing to give less than 100 per cent every time he pulls that beloved black and white shirt on.

Newcastle Evening Chronicle chief sports writer Alan Oliver has been in it right from the beginning after breaking the news of Shearer's signing from Bangkok in the summer of 1996.

Says Oliver: "It has been an absolute pleasure watching just about every game Alan Shearer has played for Newcastle United. Everyone knows about his goals. But that apart Alan Shearer is the ultimate professional. Both on and off the field. He is the perfect role model for every youngster who wants to make it in any sport. Not just football.

"This is his last season for Newcastle United and which fair-minded football fan wouldn't love to see him lift a trophy at the end of it?"

And so say all of us.

CLUB HONOURS
AND RECORDS

FOUNDED AS NEWCASTLE EAST END 1882

Football League Champions:	1905, 1907, 1909, 1927
FA Premier League Runners-up:	**1996, 1997**
Football League Division One champions:	1993
Football League Division Two champions:	**1965**
Football League promotion:	1898, 1948, 1984
FA Cup Winners:	**1910, 1924, 1932, 1951, 1952, 1955**
FA Cup runners-up:	1905, 1906, 1908, 1911, 1974, 1998, 1999
FL Cup runners-up:	**1976**
FA Charity Shield winners:	1909
FA Charity Shield runners-up:	**1933, 1952, 1953, 1956, 1996**
Sheriff of London Charity Shield winners:	1907
Inter Cities Fairs Cup winners:	**1969**
ICFC/UEFA Cup entry:	1968/69, 1969/70, 1970/71, 1977/78, 1994/95, 1996/97, 1999/00, 2003/04, 2004/05
European Champions League entry:	**1997/98, 2002/03**
European Cup Winners Cup entry:	1998/99

Record attendance:	**68,386 v Chelsea, 3 September 1930**
Record average attendance:	56,229 – Season 1947-48 (Division 2)
Record victory:	**13-0 v Newport County (H) October 1946**
Record defeat:	0-9 v Burton WDS (A) April 1895
Most league and cup goals in a career:	**200 by Jackie Milburn 1946-57**
Most league and cup goals in a season:	41 by Andy Cole 1993-94
Most league and cup appearances in a career:	**496 by Jimmy Lawrence 1904-22**
Most capped player:	Shay Given, 51 caps for Republic of Ireland, 1997-2005
Youngest player:	**Steve Watson, 16 years 223 days (November 1990 v Wolves)**
Youngest scorer:	Jackie Rutherford, 17 years 109 days (March 1902 v Bolton)
Oldest player:	**William Hampson, 44 years 225 days (April 1927 v Birmingham)**
Longest serving players:	Bill McCracken (1904-23), Frank Hudspeth (1910-29) Both 19 yrs
Record transfer fee received:	**£13.65m from Real Madrid for Jonathan Woodgate (2004)**
Record transfer fee paid:	£15m to Blackburn Rovers for Alan Shearer (1996)

First league game played by Newcastle United at St James' Park in Football League Division 2 was on 30 September 1893 v Woolwich Arsenal (won 6-0)

PLAYER PROFILES

SHOLA AMEOBI

Born:	12/10/81, Zaria, Nigeria
Position:	Striker
Previous clubs:	None

A former England Under-21 international, Shola Ameobi is on the fringes of Sven Goran Eriksson's full squad. Nigeria-born Ameobi, who came up through Newcastle United's ranks, made his debut against Chelsea as an 18-year-old and by the end of the 2004/05 season had 32 first team goals to his name. Having proved his consistent power, accuracy and skill, Ameobi is a player that few Premiership defenders enjoy marking. Brought into the first team by Sir Bobby Robson, Ameobi is rated very highly by his successor Graeme Souness.

CELESTINE BABAYARO

Born:	29/8/78, Kaduna, Nigeria
Position:	Left back
Previous clubs:	Anderlecht, Chelsea

A January transfer window signing last season, left back Celestine Babayaro replaced the outgoing Olivier Bernard. Chelsea boss Jose Mourinho had allowed Babayaro to leave Stamford Bridge in search of first team football. He made his debut at non-league Yeading in the third round of the FA Cup, and scored against Coventry City at St James' Park in the next round. His appearances, however, were limited due to injury for the rest of the season, though he returned for the final two games.

JEAN ALAIN BOUMSONG

Born:	14/12/79, Douala, Cameroon
Position:	Central defence
Previous clubs:	Le Havre, Auxerre, Rangers

SIGNED from Glasgow Rangers in last season's January transfer window, Jean Alain Boumsong did not take long to show why Graeme Souness was so keen to bring him to St James' Park. The Frenchman is a cultured defender, and an ideal partner for team-mate Titus Bramble in the heart of Newcastle United's defence. Boumsong, who collected a Scottish Premier League winner's medal for his part in Rangers' title triumph last season, is a leader both on and off the pitch and he will be a key figure for the Magpies in the 2005/06 campaign.

LEE BOWYER

Born: 3/1/77, Canning Town, London
Position: Midfield
Previous clubs: Charlton Athletic, Leeds Utd, West Ham United

RESTORED to his favoured central midfield role, Lee Bowyer flourished for much of the 2004/05 season. The Londoner had started out at Charlton Athletic before his big-money move to Leeds United in the summer of 1996. Bowyer starred in Leeds' run in the Champions League of 2000/01, contributing vital goals as David O'Leary's team reached the semi finals. After a brief spell with his boyhood heroes West Ham United, Sir Bobby Robson snapped Bowyer up on a free transfer in July 2003.

TITUS BRAMBLE

Born: 31/7/81, Ipswich
Position: Central defence
Previous clubs: Ipswich Town

TITUS Bramble showed in the second half of the 2004/05 season why Sir Bobby Robson paid £5m for him in the summer of 2002. A powerful defender, Bramble has all the physical attributes to make it to the top of the game. The former Ipswich Town player was badly missed when he underwent a groin operation midway through last season, with the surgery having come just as he was hitting the best form of his Magpies career. Bramble will be hoping to make up for lost time this season.

MARTIN BRITTAIN

Born:	29/12/84, Newcastle
Position:	Midfield
Previous clubs:	None

BRITTAIN has been associated with Newcastle United since the age of nine, coming up through the junior ranks before making his team debut in March 2004 against Valerenga in the UEFA Cup. He was an ever-present for the Magpies' Under-17s in the 2001/02 season when they won the national play-offs. The next season Brittain made his Premiership Reserve League debut against Liverpool and impressed Sir Bobby Robson with the way he settled into the second string. Brittain received the Wor Jackie award from Sport Newcastle in 2004, awarded annually to one of the club's most promising youngsters.

STEPHEN CARR

Born:	29/8/76, Dublin
Position:	Right back
Previous clubs:	Tottenham Hotspur

AN attack-minded right back, Stephen Carr made 39 appearances for Newcastle United in his first season at St James' Park. Carr had been looking for a new challenge having spent more than a decade at Tottenham Hotspur. Sir Bobby Robson paid £2m to unite Carr with his Republic of Ireland team-mates Shay Given and Andy O'Brien, and the Dubliner had a successful first season on Tyneside. Carr scored a spectacular winner for the Magpies at Southampton as newly-installed Graeme Souness guided his new club to their first away league win over the Saints in 32 years.

MICHAEL CHOPRA

Born:	23/12/83, Newcastle
Position:	Forward
Previous clubs:	Watford (loan), Nottingham Forest (loan), Barnsley (loan)

CHOPRA has long been one of Newcastle United's brightest prospects, and the former England Under-21 international faces his biggest season yet at St James' Park. Chopra has had spells on loan at Watford, Nottingham Forest and Barnsley during his Magpies career. In 2004/05 the striker spent the season on loan at Barnsley and scored 17 goals for the League One club. His reward was a new one-year contract, with Graeme Souness promising Chopra he would be given a chance to prove he could score goals for his hometown club at the highest level.

KIERON DYER

Born:	29/12/78, Ipswich
Position:	Midfield
Previous clubs:	Ipswich Town

THE England international rediscovered his best form under Graeme Souness in the 2003/04 season. But the campaign ended in frustration for Dyer, who had scored six goals. Dyer missed the last four games of the season after aggravating the hamstring injury he suffered in Newcastle United's UEFA Cup quarter final against Sporting Lisbon. The former Ipswich Town midfielder showed his versatility through the season, playing across the midfield as well as up front for Souness. He also turned out at right back at Aston Villa.

ROBBIE ELLIOTT

Born:	25/12/73, Gosforth, Newcastle
Postion:	Left back
Previous clubs:	Newcastle United, Bolton Wanderers

THE Gosforth-born player agreed a new contract with Newcastle United late in the 2004/05 season. Elliott, in his second spell at the club, had seemed to be on his way out of St James' Park at the start of the campaign, having not played a competitive first team game for 20 months. However he was pressed into action away to Middlesbrough by Sir Bobby Robson, and the defender went on to to make a total of 22 appearances. Graeme Souness rewarded Elliott for his contribution to the cause with a year's extension to his contract.

AMADY FAYE

Born:	12/3/77, Dakar, Senegal
Postion:	Midfield
Previous clubs:	Auxerre, Portsmouth

SIGNED from Portsmouth in the January transfer window by Graeme Souness, Amady Faye was introduced to St James' Park as a specialist defensive midfielder. With Nicky Butt out of the team injured, and Gary Speed having departed Newcastle United during the previous summer, Souness felt it was a position that particularly needed strengthening if the Magpies were to tighten up away from home. Faye went on to make 17 appearances for his new club before his season was ended early by injury.

SHAY GIVEN

Born: 20/4/76, Lifford, County Donegal
Position: Goalkeeper
Previous clubs: Celtic, Blackburn Rovers, Swindon Town (loan), Sunderland (loan)

ARGUABLY the Premiership's top goalkeeper, Shay Given has gone from strength to strength since joining Newcastle United from Blackburn Rovers. The 2004/05 season was Given's eighth at St James' Park, during which he has only missed a handful of games. Given's remarkable record of 140 consecutive Premiership appearances was broken last season as his wife was giving birth while the Magpies took on Fulham. He has also been a model of consistency for the Republic of Ireland and his performances at the 2002 World Cup marked him out as one of the best goalkeepers in the world.

STEVE HARPER

Born: 14/3/75, Easington, County Durham
Position: Goalkeeper
Previous clubs: Seaham Red Star

UNDERSTUDY to Shay Given for much of his Newcastle United career, Steve Harper would walk into plenty of Premiership sides. Given's form between the posts, and his remarkable run without serious injury, has limited Harper's appearances. He made five starts and a further two appearances as substitute in the 2004/05 season, and he will be hoping for a change of luck this season having ditched his "unlucky" No. 13 jersey in 2004. Easington-born Harper had been signed from non-league side Seaham Red Star, before rising through the club's ranks.

JERMAINE JENAS

Born: 18/2/83, Nottingham
Position: Midfield
Previous clubs: Nottingham Forest

THE fact that Jermaine Jenas was handed the captaincy during Alan Shearer's absence through injury in the 2004/05 season showed the faith that Graeme Souness has in the midfielder. Jenas became the most expensive 18-year-old in world football when he joined Newcastle United for £5m in early 2002. The fee eclipsed the £4m that PSV Eindhoven paid for Brazilian striker Ronaldo in 1994, but the deal now looks a bargain. Souness believes Jenas, now a regular in Sven Goran Eriksson's England squad, has the potential to be "the best midfield player in Europe".

JAMES MILNER

Born: 4/1/86, Leeds
Position: Midfield
Previous clubs: Leeds Utd, Swindon Town (loan)

JAMES Milner suffered the heartbreak of relegation with his hometown club Leeds United in 2003/04. Leeds' drop down to the Championship forced the Elland Road club to sell its best players, and the teenage midfielder was quickly signed up by Newcastle United on a five-year contract. Versatile Milner can play across the midfield, as well as up front, and he showed what he could do with a late-season run in Graeme Souness' team. Now Milner will be hoping to secure a regular first team place under Souness.

CHARLES N'ZOGBIA

Born:	28/5/86, Harfleur, France
Position:	Midfield
Previous clubs:	Le Havre

FRENCH teenager Charles N'Zogbia joined up with Newcastle United for pre-season training in 2004/05, and impressed then manager Sir Bobby Robson so much that he signed the midfielder. After a contractual dispute with N'Zogbia's former club Le Havre was settled in the Magpies' favour, he was cleared to play for his new club. The left-footed player enjoyed a run in the team late in the season during an injury crisis, and N'Zogbia performed well both in the centre and on the left side of midfield. By the end of the campaign he had made 19 appearances for the club.

PETER RAMAGE

Born:	22/11/83, Ashington
Position:	Central defence
Previous clubs:	None

HOME-GROWN defender Peter Ramage committed himself to three more years at Newcastle United at the end of the 2004/05 season. A product of the club's Academy, Ramage made his full debut against Manchester United at Old Trafford. Ramage was playing out of position at right back against Ryan Giggs, but the Ashington-born player turned in an impressive performance against one of the best left wingers in the game. Now he will be looking to build on his breakthrough season by challenging regularly for a first team place in 2005/06.

ALAN SHEARER

Born: 13/8/70, Gosforth, Newcastle
Position: Forward
Previous clubs: Southampton, Blackburn Rovers

ARGUABLY the greatest English goalscorer of his generation, Alan Shearer has passed milestone after milestone since joining his hometown club for a world-record fee of £15m in 1996. Shearer ended the 2004/05 season just eight goals short of Jackie Milburn's all-time record of 200 goals. The former England captain had been planning to retire at the end of that campaign, but was persuaded to play on by Graeme Souness. Shearer will be hoping his last season in a black and white shirt will see Newcastle United finally win some silverware, with the Magpies having gone close several times in his St James' Park career.

STEVEN TAYLOR

Born: 23/1/86, Greenwich, London
Position: Central defence
Previous clubs: None

STEVEN Taylor's breakthrough into Graeme Souness' team was undoubtedly the defining success story of the 2004/05 season. The 19-year-old defender, who had made a couple of appearances in the previous season under former manager Sir Bobby Robson, was thrown in at the deep end playing right back against Everton in November – and never looked back. Taylor also got the opportunity to play in his favoured position of centre half, and continued his progress at England Under-21 level.

WORD SEARCH

This is a tough one! See if you can find the surnames of 25 of Newcastle United's Premiership heroes hidden within this wordsearch.

```
B Q M F L R M G S E H G U H K R M
A B X L D Z G H N K R A L C W X G
R D N R J E R P E A C O C K W N B
T R W L R E E S L T N G C J O L J
O R Q G R T A P V M N F I S L M J
N Y E A C Z N N S V E Q U N G R L
M W E B I X Q K E R L G F I O N N
M H J B L B Y N D Y R K L I D L R
S L A X W A I I Z E T L J B R N A
S D A R X S N N F L E L H O O F T
O W S H O A E K V S M T Y E F N X
L G P N N V N N P D T B M M S I G
A V R D I X F I M R C L A A E F R
N Z I G B W E M C A Y O L B R F K
O E L L I O T T L E E V L V E I N
L G L R H G P B B B L G E E B R Q
L Z A T R S R N I C E K B F M G V
```

Answers on p61

42

FA CUP REVIEW

WHEN Newcastle United started their FA Cup campaign in 2004-05 they knew it was exactly 50 years since they last won the prestigious trophy. And they had a go at putting this right, reaching the semi-final before running out of steam and players.

Yet when they drew non-league Yeading in the third round it evoked memories of that embarrasing defeat by Hereford over 30 years earlier. Not many Newcastle fans had heard of Yeading when the draw was made. Or what League they played in.

Yeading's ground was soon ruled out as being unsuitable and the tie was staged at Queens Park Rangers' Loftus Road. Not surprisingly there was massive media interest but as soon as Lee Bowyer put Newcastle in front in the 51st minute it was all over bar the shouting and Shola Ameobi made the final scoreline 2-0.

What Newcastle needed after all this was a straightforward fourth round tie. And they got it when they were drawn against Championship outfit Coventry City at St James' Park. And sure enough Newcastle ran out 3-1 winners in a low key game with Celestine Babayaro scoring his first goal for the club. This brought Chelsea - who had already knocked Newcastle out of Carling Cup in extra time at St James' Park - back to Tyneside and in a game that had everything United emerged 1-0 winners.

Patrick Kluivert scored the only goal of the game when he headed in Laurent Robert's fourth minute cross to see Graeme Souness's side storm into the quarters-finals. At the time everyone knew that Chelsea were probably on their way to the Premiership title. But probably what no-one could have guessed that cold February afternoon was that Newcastle would inflict Chelsea with their only domestic defeat of the year. What Newcastle wanted most of all was a third successive home FA Cup draw. And

they got it when they were paired with Spurs at St James' Park for a place in the semi-finals. And for the first time in their history Newcastle were still involved in two cup competitions in March as they were still going strong in the UEFA Cup. And March was to become April as Newcastle gained revenge for an earlier Premiership defeat in front of their home supporters by Spurs with a 1-0 victory.

Once again an early goal from Patrick Kluivert was enough to do the trick as Newcastle marched into the semi-finals of the FA Cup. And Newcastle fans got their first ever visit to Cardiff's Millennium Stadium for their FA Cup semi-final with Manchester United. But it came just a couple of days after Newcastle had an energy-sapping visit to Portugal where they were knocked out of the UEFA Cup by Sporting Lisbon. In contrast the Reds had a free week to prepare for the semi-final and it showed as Manchester United roared into a 3-0 lead. However most of the roaring came from the Newcastle fans in what many believe was their finest hour in the way they supported their team.

At least those fans had something to cheer when Shola Ameobi pulled a goal back in the 59th minute. But Ronaldo restored Manchester United's three goal advantage with a fourth goal against a rapidly tiring Newcastle. As Newcastle dragged their weary limbs off at the end of the game they knew they had given their all to try to bring a cup to Tyneside in 2004-5.

The Cardiff semi-final was their 19th cup game of the season. They won 15 of them, only losing on the three occasions when they went out to Chelsea in the Carling Cup, Sporting Lisbon in the UEFA Cup and Manchester United in the FA Cup. Over the season they actually scored twice as many goals in cup competitions as they conceded. But this was no consolation as they and their magnificent fans made the long trek home from Cardiff.

RESULTS

THIRD ROUND:

YEADING 0 NEWCASTLE 2
(9.01.05 Bowyer, Ameobi)

FOURTH ROUND:

NEWCASTLE 3 COVENTRY CITY 1
(29.01.05 Shearer, Ameobi, Babayaro)

FIFTH ROUND:

NEWCASTLE 1 CHELSEA 0
(20.02.05 Kluivert)

SIXTH ROUND:

NEWCASTLE 1 SPURS 0
(13.03.05 Kluivert)

SEMI-FINAL:

NEWCASTLE 1 MANCHESTER UTD 4
(17.04.05 Ameobi)

JUNIOR MAGPIES ASKS...

" HOW DO YOU SUPPORT THE TOON? "

ALWAYS WEAR YOUR 'LUCKY' SOCKS TO THE MATCH?
CHEER THE LOUDEST WHEN UNITED SCORE?
HAVE THE MOST NUFC PENCILS IN YOUR WHOLE SCHOOL?

OR... **JOIN THE JUNIOR MAGPIES!**

The Official Newcastle United Supporters Club for Under 16s

WE'RE here to help make YOU a part of the action here at St James' Park. Whether you live in Gateshead or Grimsby you can help support the lads throughout the 05/06 Season by joining Junior Magpies. With Junior Magpies you not only get involved with your favourite team but you also benefit from all this great stuff...

- A wicked membership pack on joining, packed full of great goodies
- A personalised membership card and certificate
- Birthday and Christmas cards from the team
- 3 Postermags throughout the year packed full of the latest news and competitions
- The chance to apply for a place at our Xmas Parties, Autograph Session, and Away Trips
- Exclusive competitions and prizes, including our annual Away Mascots Competition
- Discounts on FITC Training Courses and Birthday Parties at St James' Park
- Free entry to Home Reserve Team Games

Junior Magpies is the biggest and best club of its kind in the Premiership so why not join us?

Membership for the 05/06 Season costs just £20 for UK members, and £23 from overseas.

FOR MORE INFORMATION OR TO APPLY TODAY: CALL US NOW ON 0191 201 8471/2 OR VISIT THE JUNIOR MAGPIE PAGES AT WWW.NUFC.CO.UK

10 FACTS ABOUT
KIERON DYER

1 He was signed for £6m from Ipswich Town on July 16, 1999

2 He made his senior England debut against Luxembourg at Wembley on September 4, 1999

3 He made three substitute appearances for England in the 2002 World Cup finals

4 His middle name is Courtney

5 He was born in Ipswich on December 29, 1978

6 He played at right back at Aston Villa in the 2004/05 season

7 He captained Newcastle United for the first time in a competitive game against Everton in the League Cup on November 6, 2002 – and scored twice

8 At the end of the 2004/05 season, he had made 207 first team appearances, and scored 28 goals, for Newcastle United

9 He made 11 appearances for England's Under-21s

10 His first goal for Newcastle United came against Sunderland at St James' Park on August 25, 1999

NEW SIGNINGS

SCOTT PARKER

Born:	13/10/84, Lambeth, London
Position:	Midfield
Previous clubs:	Charlton Athletic, Norwich City (loan), Chelsea

NEWCASTLE United pulled off one of the transfer coups of the summer when they signed Scott Parker from Premiership champions Chelsea.

Graeme Souness and his chairman Freddy Shepherd swooped once it became clear Jose Mourinho was reluctantly prepared to sell Parker, who had found his chances limited in 2004/05. Once Newcastle's bid was accepted, things moved quickly with Parker prepared to interrupt his family holiday in Portugal to sign for United. Parker and his agent Paul Martin arrived at St James' Park the night before the deal was done, with Parker staying in a club flat at the stadium after jetting into Newcastle International Airport. The 25-year-old could not resist a quick look inside the empty stadium before he got some sleep.

Parker was up first thing the next morning and had completed a medical at a Tyneside hospital by 8am. He returned to St James' to conclude talks on a five year contract.

By now Newcastle's press office was fielding enquiries from journalists, and as the clamour intensified Parker took the opportunity to visit United's state-of-the-art training ground while the club's press officer hastily arranged a media call. It was announced that a press conference would be held at the St James' Park media suite early in the afternoon once all the relevant paperwork was completed. And at 3.30pm Parker, flanked by Souness and his assistant Terry McDermott, walked into the media suite to be greeted by several dozen eager reporters, photographers and cameramen.

Shepherd took a back seat, satisfied at having landed one of the summer's most sought-after players. On the stage Parker answered questions from TV journalists and the Press, before speaking to radio reporters. "There were a lot of factors," said Parker. "The manager obviously played a role and, from the minute Newcastle showed an interest, I felt I wanted to come here.

"Next year is going to be a big year for us and I want to start building something."

After a whirlwind 24 hours on Tyneside Parker headed to the airport for a flight back to Portugal, relishing the season ahead in black and white.

EMRE BELOZOGLU

Born:	07/09/80, Istanbul, Turkey
Position:	Midfield
Previous clubs:	Inter Milan, Galatasaray

AN intervention from Turkey's Prime Minister could not stop Emre signing for Newcastle United. PM Recep Tayyip Erdogan was desperate for Belozoglu to return to his homeland once it became clear he would be allowed to leave Inter Milan after a successful spell in Italy. But the left-sided midfielder had his heart set on the Premiership – and a move to St James' Park.

Chairman Freddy Shepherd said: "Emre is a massive star – the Prime Minister of Turkey begged him to go back home from Inter Milan.

How often does a Prime Minister do that?" And manager Graeme Souness added: "There were other teams interested in Emre, and we all worked very hard to get him. He was a player very much in demand in his own country and the most successful club in Turkey at the moment, Fenerbahce, were desperate to sign him. The Turkish Prime Minister also got involved and tried to persuade him to stay in his own country, and AC, the other big club in Milan, were interested in taking him as well."

Emre - the David Beckham of Turkish football - became the first ever Turkish player to join Newcastle United when he signed a five-year deal with the club in July 2005.

He had joined Galatasaray in his native Istanbul at the age of 15, when Souness was in charge, and made his debut a year later. Emre scored a dramatic winner in a 3-2 win over arch rivals Besiktas which won his team the league title in 1996-97, and made his Champions League debut aged 17 the following season.

After seven trophies in five seasons with Galatasaray, he joined Serie A club Inter along with team-mates Okan and Haka Sukur. Emre went on to play in three Champions League campaigns for Inter, including the 2002-03 season when the San Siro club were paired with the Magpies in the second group stage.

At international level, he played a major part in Turkey's run to the semi-finals of the World Cup in 2002. Emre can play on the left side of midfield, through the middle or off a striker, with the 24-year-old's versatility one of his biggest assets.

He is also a hard worker, with Souness believing his game combines grit and determination with attacking flair.

GRAEME SOUNESS

GRAEME SOUNESS was a surprise choice as Sir Bobby Robson's successor at St James' Park.

The bookmakers had Souness as an outsider for one of the biggest jobs in football - not that the Scot minded. He was happy to be managing a club of the size and stature of Newcastle United. Souness had been at Blackburn Rovers for more than four years, guiding the Lancashire club to the Worthington Cup in 2002. Former Magpies striker Andy Cole scored the winner for Blackburn at Cardiff's Millennium Stadium, and the cup was just the latest of many won during a long and successful managerial career.

It had started at Glasgow Rangers, where Souness was appointed player-manager in 1986. He led the Ibrox club to three League titles and four League Cups. Souness then succeeded Kenny Dalglish at Liverpool and he returned from heart surgery ahead of the FA Cup final in 1992, with the Reds going on to beat Sunderland at Wembley.

He left Anfield in 1994 and the following year was appointed manager of Istanbul club Galatasaray. He guided them to the Turkish Cup.

Souncess then had a spell at Southampton, saving the south coast club from relegation from the Premiership.

His next managerial post was at Benfica, Souness joining the Portuguese club in 1997. Souness, however, was back in England two years later and in 2000 he was appointed Blackburn boss.

Now on Tyneside, Souness is determined to bring silverware to St James', having been a winner throughout his playing and managerial careers. He had started out at Tottenham Hotspur, but it was at Middlesbrough where he made his name. Souness quickly earned a reputation as a tough-tackling, and ball-playing, midfielder. He made 176 appearances for the Teesside club, helping them win promotion to the top flight, before signing for Liverpool in a £350,000 deal in 1978. At Anfield, Souness won five League titles, three European Cups and four League Cups.

He joined Italian club Sampdoria in 1984, and two years later returned to his native Scotland to take over at Rangers.

Full name:
Graeme James Souness

Born:
May 6, 1953, Edinburgh

Height:
5ft 11

Playing career:
Tottenham Hotspur, Middlesbrough, Liverpool, Sampdoria, Glasgow Rangers

International career:
54 caps

Managerial career:
Glasgow Rangers, Liverpool, Galatasaray, Southampton, Torino, Benfica, Blackburn Rovers

Managerial honours:
Scottish League 1987, 1989 and 1990.
Scottish League Cup 1987, 1988, 1989 and 1991.
English FA Cup 1992.
Turkish Cup 1996.
English League Cup 2002.

CROSSWORD

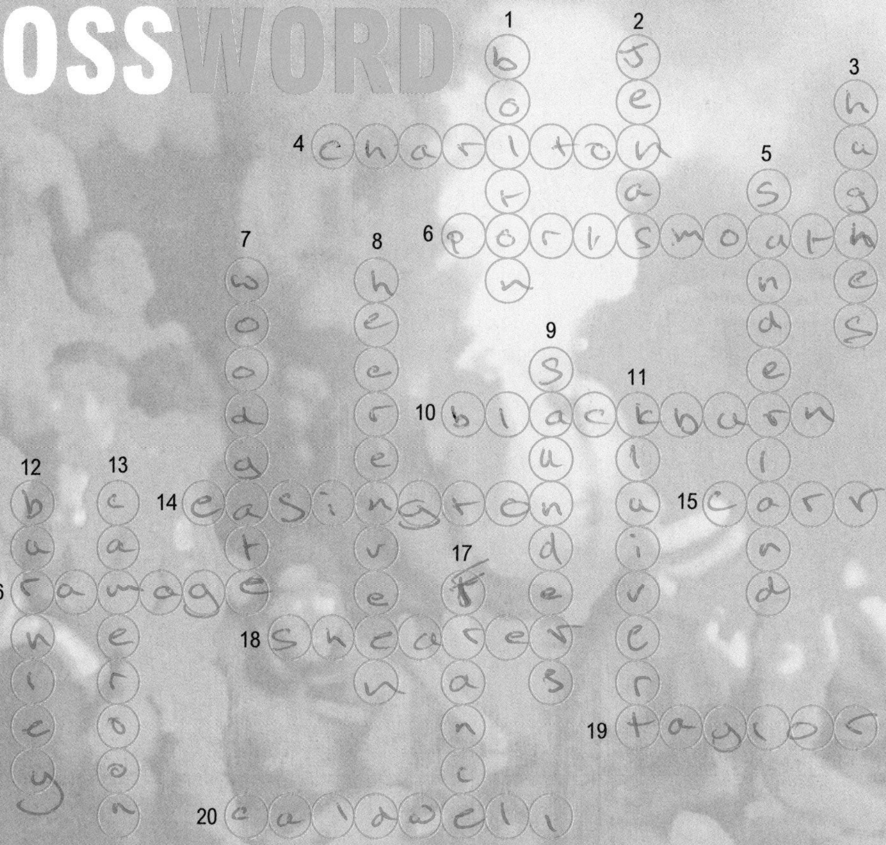

ACROSS

4 At which London club did Newcastle United midfielder Scott Parker start his professional career?

6 From which club did Newcastle United sign midfielder Amady Faye?

10 From which club did Newcastle United sign goalkeeper Shay Given?

14 Where was goalkeeper Steve Harper born?

15 Which Newcastle United player scored the winner at Southampton in the 04/05 season?

16 Which Newcastle United player made his full debut away to Manchester United in the 2004/05 campaign?

18 Name Newcastle United's top scorer in the 2004/05 season.

19 Which England Under-21 defender made 22 appearances for Newcastle United last season?

20 Which player left Newcastle United for Tyne-Wear rivals Sunderland in June 2004?

DOWN

1 Robbie Elliott played for which club between his two spells at Newcastle United?

2 Which Newcastle United player went on England's tour to the United States at the end of the 2004/05 season?

3 Newcastle United sold which long-serving defender to Aston Villa in May 2005?

5 While at Leeds United, James Milner became the youngest scorer in Premiership history by scoring against which club?

7 Newcastle United sold which player to Real Madrid for £13.4m in August 2004?

8 Name the Dutch club that Newcastle United knocked out of the UEFA Cup in the 2004/05 campaign.

9 Name Graeme Souness' first team coach.

11 Who scored the winner for Newcastle United against Chelsea in the FA Cup in the 2004/05 campaign?

12 Michael Chopra scored four goals in one game while on loan for Watford in the 2002/03 season. Name the opposition.

13 Name the country of Jean Alain Boumsong's birth?

17 Midfielder Charles N'Zogbia was born in which country?

Answers on p61

BACKROOM STAFF

ALAN MURRAY
Assistant to the manager

Alan Murray has known Graeme Souness since their days together at Middlesbrough in the 1970s, and has been his assistant for the best part of a decade. Murray's playing career took him to Wolverhampton Wanderers, Brenford and Doncaster Rovers as well as Boro. After he hung up his boots Alan - a Geordie who was born and bred in Walker - went on to have spells in charge of North East clubs Hartlepool United and Doncaster before he teamed up with Souness. The 2004/05 season was Murray's 35th in professional football.

TERRY McDERMOTT
Assistant to the manager

Graeme Souness is the third Newcastle United manager that Terry McDermott has worked with, having been assistant to both Kevin Keegan and Kenny Dalglish in the 1990s. Twice a player at the club, McDermott's fourth spell at St James' Park started in February 2005 when he was appointed as assistant to the manager. He joined the Magpies from Bury in February 1973 and moved on to Liverpool in late 1974. After winning domestic and European honours at Anfield, McDermott returned to St James' to team up with Keegan, a former Anfield team-mate.

DEAN SAUNDERS
First team coach

Graeme Souness worked with striker Dean Saunders three times during the Welshman's playing career, taking him to Liverpool, Galatasaray and Benfica. Saunders joined Souness' backroom staff at Blackburn Rovers when he called time on his playing career. Now first team coach under Souness at Newcastle United, Saunders takes a special interest in the Magpies' strikers having plundered more than 250 goals during his long career. Saunders also had spells at Derby County and Aston Villa among others, and won 75 caps for Wales.

ROY TUNKS
Goalkeeping coach

Roy Tunks joined Newcastle United as goalkeeping coach from Blackburn Rovers a month after Graeme Souness' appointment at St James' Park, having been at Ewood Park since 1997. Tunks had turned out in goal for Wigan Athletic, Preston North End, York City and Rotherham United in a long playing career. He also nearly turned out for Newcastle United, having been at St James' Park on loan from Rotherham in the early to mid-1970s. Tunks made three reserve appearances for the Magpies in the Central League at the start of the 1974/75 season.

UNDER 18s

NEWCASTLE United has a proud history of developing its own players – and the Magpies are investing heavily in the next generation of footballing talent. Homegrown duo Shola Ameobi and Steven Taylor came up through the club's Academy and are now established Premiership players.

The Academy facility at Little Benton adjoins the first team's training ground and offers state-of-the-art facilities. The next generation of talent is benefiting from that investment, with several young players currently making a name for themselves in the club's Reserve and Under-18s teams. Former Newcastle United players Tommy Craig, Glenn Roeder, Peter Beardsley and Kenny Wharton work with the club's future stars.

Craig is the club's Reserve Team Coach, while Roeder returned to the North East for the 2005/06 season as Academy Manager, working alongside coaches Beardsley and Wharton.

Last season the Magpies Under-18s had a tremendous campaign and won Group D of the FA Premier Academy League, which put them into the national play-offs. And Roeder, Beardsley and Wharton will be looking to build on that success in the 2005/06 campaign, while Craig will continue to blood youngsters into the club's Reserve team. Among the prospects at Newcastle United is England Under-18 central defender Paul Huntington, who collected Sport Newcastle's Wor Jackie Award in March 2005.

The award is presented annually to the club's brightest prospects, and the Carlisle-born player is certainly one to watch. Forward Marc Walton, a prolific scorer at Academy level, has also represented England's Under-18s. Defender David Edgar, whose father Eddie was once a goalkeeper at the club, has played for Canada at Under-19 level.

South Africa-born Matty Pattison saw his 2004/05 season wrecked by injury, but the talented midfielder, who played for the first team in a friendly at Celtic in August 2004, is determined to bounce back.

Goalkeeper Ben Smith hopes to follow in his hero Shay Given's footsteps and make the first team, while South Shields-born striker Carl Finnigan idolises Alan Shearer. Finnigan found the net three times in the FA Premiership Reserve League in 2004/05.

TOMMY CRAIG — Reserve team coach

Once the most expensive teenager in football, Tommy Craig went on to spend four years at St James' Park in the 1970s. The Scot, a left-footed midfielder, had the honour of captaining Newcastle United in the 1976 League Cup final. Kenny Dalglish brought Craig back to Newcastle United in April 1998 to fulfil the role of reserve team coach.

GLENN ROEDER — Academy manager

Famed for his "shuffle" during his playing days, Glenn Roeder was a cultured central defender. Roeder spent most of his five-and-a-half years at Newcastle United as captain, playing alongside the likes of Kevin Keegan and Paul Gascoigne. The former West Ham United and Watford manager rejoined his old club in June 2005.

PETER BEARDSLEY — Academy coach

Widely-regarded as one of the greatest ever players to pull on the black and white of Newcastle United, striker Peter Beardsley had two playing spells at St James' Park. Now Beardsley is passing on his immense knowledge to the club's next generation as an Academy coach.

KENNY WHARTON — Academy coach

Tough-tackling defender Kenny Wharton spent more than a decade a St James' Park during his playing career, making a remarkable 335 appearances between 1978-89. After a spell coaching at Middlesbrough, Wharton returned to Newcastle United to coach at the club's Academy.

NEWCASTLE UNITED'S
TOP PREMIERSHIP GOALS

1 ALAN SHEARER v Manchester City (a)

Alan Shearer's 250th Premiership goal came against Manchester City, whose manager Kevin Keegan signed him for Newcastle United back in the summer of 1996. Shearer's strike at the City of Manchester Stadium ranked up there with his very best. He latched onto Titus Bramble's diagonal ball before racing to the box and lashing a stunning shot past David James.

2 DARREN AMBROSE v Bolton Wanderers (a)

After El Haji Diouf sent Bolton Wanderers into the lead in the 52nd minute it looked like it would take something special to get the Magpies back into the game at the Reebok Stadium. Three minutes later Darren Ambrose provided it. He picked the ball up in the Bolton half, turned inside Gary Speed and Ian Nolan and then unleashed an unstoppable 25-yard shot past Jussi Jaaskelainen.

3 STEPHEN CARR v Southampton (a)

In his first Premiership game under Graeme Souness, Stephen Carr was clearly out to impress his new manager. He scored the winner as Newcastle United ended their 32-year wait for a win at Southampton. With the score at 1-1, Jermaine Jenas rolled a free kick to Carr and the full back struck a swerving 30-yard right-foot shot past a stunned Saints goalkeeper Antti Niemi at St Mary's Stadium.

4 LAURENT ROBERT v Liverpool (h)

Laurent Robert made a habit of scoring against Liverpool during his Newcastle United career, and the former wingman brought St James' Park to its feet with another spectacular free kick. After Alan Shearer was pulled back by Mauricio Pellegrino, Robert stepped up to take the resulting set piece. He curled it past Scott Carson with his left foot to give the Magpies the victory.

5 NICKY BUTT v Birmingham City (a)

During his long association with Manchester United Nicky Butt rarely grabbed the headlines for his goalscoring, but early in his Newcastle United career he showed he could find the net. James Milner crossed from the right and with Birmingham City appealing for a foul by Alan Shearer, Butt scored from 15 yards with a spectacular scissors kick to level the scores at St Andrews.

SEASON 2004/2005...

6 ALAN SHEARER v Manchester United (h)

This was to be the last St James' Park saw of Alan Shearer for two months, with Newcastle United's captain going on to miss a chunk of the campaign with a niggling muscle injury. Shearer turned Wes Brown and with strike partner Craig Bellamy pulling defenders out of position he went inside before turning and striking a sweet left foot shot past Roy Carroll in the Manchester United goal.

7 DARREN AMBROSE v Manchester Utd (a)

Darren Ambrose silenced Old Trafford with his 27th minute opening goal, the home fans having been expecting a Manchester United breakthrough against Graeme Souness' makeshift and youthful team. Ambrose intercepted Tim Howard's poor clearance and after exchanging passes with Shola Ameobi he jinked past Gabriel Heinze and Wes Brown before slotting the ball into the bottom corner.

8 LAURENT ROBERT v Manchester City (h)

Laurent Robert does not seem to score tap-ins, and the goal that opened the scoring against Kevin Keegan's Manchester was another one to remember from the Frenchman. After Paul Bosvelt brought down Nicky Butt four minutes into the second half, Robert stepped up and curled a superb 25-yard free kick inside David James' left-hand post.

9 LEE BOWYER v Portsmouth (h)

A challenge from Lee Bowyer on former Newcastle United striker Lomana LuaLua in the centre circle went unpunished, allowing Steven Taylor to race forward before slipping the ball to Bowyer. The midfielder continued his own run and lashed a 20-yard shot past Portsmouth goalkeeper Jamie Ashdown, going on to celebrate in front of the fans in the Sir John Hall Stand.

10 PATRICK KLUIVERT v Crystal Palace (a)

Patrick Kluivert produced a moment of skill to light up a cold and wet Selhurst Park, with his cheeky back heel opening the scoring against Crystal Palace in the 79th minute. For all their possession in the second half, it had been looking like Newcastle United would never score until Craig Bellamy raced down the right and crossed for Kluivert, who back-heeled the ball past Gabor Kiraly.

DID YOU KNOW?

Peter Ramage's dad Ian is an international rugby union referee, and has served as a touch judge in the last two World Cups.

Shola Ameobi's younger brother Tomi is at Newcastle United's Academy.

Robbie Elliott was born on Christmas Day.

Titus Bramble's brother Tes is also a professional footballer. He has played for Southend United and Cambridge United.

James Milner broke Wayne Rooney's record as the youngest-ever Premiership scorer by four days when he scored for Leeds United against Sunderland aged 16 and 357 days. Everton's James Vaughan now holds the record.

Steve Harper changed his squad number from 13 to 12 in 2003 - because he felt it was unlucky.

Jean Alain Boumsong is a big fan of classical music.

Alan Shearer is the Premiership's all-time leading goalscorer with the striker having scored 250 goals up to the end of the 2004/05 season.

Steven Taylor was born in London but moved to Whitley Bay when he was only a few days old and considers himself a Geordie.

Steve Harper is a qualified referee and used to officiate Sunday League games.

QUIZ ANSWERS

QUIZ 1: PLAYERS

1 Ipswich Town
2 Nigeria
3 Shay Given
4 Jermaine Jenas
5 Rangers
6 Senegal
7 Bolton Wanderers
8 Stephen Carr
9 Titus Bramble
10 French

QUIZ 2: EUROPE

1 Sochaux
2 Shay Given
3 True
4 Steven Taylor
5 Sporting Lisbon
6 Three times: 1997-98, 2002-3 and 2003-4
7 Shola Ameobi
8 Peter Ramage
9 Marseille
10 Feyenoord

QUIZ 3: STRIKERS

1 Faustino Asprilla
2 Derby County
3 John Dahl Tomasson
4 Wimbledon
5 14
6 1993/94
7 Coventry City
8 Darren Huckerby
9 Barnsley
10 Carl Cort
11 Everton
12 CSKA Sofia
13 Peter Beardsley
14 Lomana Lualua
15 Malcolm Allen

CROSSWORD

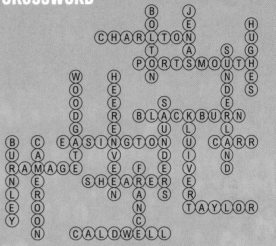

WORD SEARCH

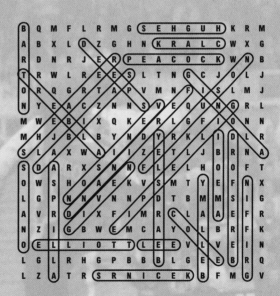

HOW MANY DID YOU GET RIGHT?